Great Danes as Pets

A Complete Great Danes Pet Owner's Guide

Great Danes breeding, where to buy, types, care, temperament, cost, health, handling, diet, and much more included!

By: Lolly Brown

Copyrights and Trademarks

All rights reserved. No part of this book may be reproduced or transformed in any form or by any means, graphic, electronic, or mechanical, including photocopying, recording, taping, or by any information storage retrieval system, without the written permission of the author.

This publication is Copyright ©2018 NRB Publishing, an imprint. Nevada. All products, graphics, publications, software and services mentioned and recommended in this publication are protected by trademarks. In such instance, all trademarks & copyright belong to the respective owners. For information consult www.NRBpublishing.com

Disclaimer and Legal Notice

This product is not legal, medical, or accounting advice and should not be interpreted in that manner. You need to do your own due-diligence to determine if the content of this product is right for you. While every attempt has been made to verify the information shared in this publication, neither the author, neither publisher, nor the affiliates assume any responsibility for errors, omissions or contrary interpretation of the subject matter herein. Any perceived slights to any specific person(s) or organization(s) are purely unintentional.

We have no control over the nature, content and availability of the web sites listed in this book. The inclusion of any web site links does not necessarily imply a recommendation or endorse the views expressed within them. We take no responsibility for, and will not be liable for, the websites being temporarily unavailable or being removed from the internet.

The accuracy and completeness of information provided herein and opinions stated herein are not guaranteed or warranted to produce any particular results, and the advice and strategies, contained herein may not be suitable for every individual. Neither the author nor the publisher shall be liable for any loss incurred as a consequence of the use and application, directly or indirectly, of any information presented in this work. This publication is designed to provide information in regard to the subject matter covered.

Neither the author nor the publisher assume any responsibility for any errors or omissions, nor do they represent or warrant that the ideas, information, actions, plans, suggestions contained in this book is in all cases accurate. It is the reader's responsibility to find advice before putting anything written in this book into practice. The information in this book is not intended to serve as legal, medical, or accounting advice.

Foreword

Dogs are one of the most common household pets you can have. You may automatically want a small breed because it is easy to take care of and more loving, but you might opt to look at big breeds.

Great Danes may look intimidating at first, due to its height and built, but under their majestic appearance, they have marvellous attitudes and traits that you would really love! Great Danes have amazing traits that would be a real attention; people would be star - struck if they knew you are the owner of this amazing breed.

Read on to know more about this breed. We will provide you with lots of information regarding its rich history, temperament, activity, taking care of puppies, and training it. This book will equip you with necessary knowledge to take care of your dream pet. Make sure you do not skip a chapter so you will not miss anything! Have fun reading!

Table of Contents

Introduction 1
Chapter One: Let's Start With the Basics 2
   General Appearance and Showmanship Qualities 3
   Height 8
   Weight 9
   Lifespan 9
   Diet and Feeding 9
      Feeding Your Puppy 10
      Feeding an Adult Dog 11
   Health 12
   Personality and Temperament 13
      Quick Facts 15
Chapter Two: Taking Care of Your Great Dane 18
   What Makes It a Great Pet 19
   Where to Purchase your Great Dane 19
   Tell Tale Signs of a Reputable Breeder 22
   Characteristics of a Healthy Breed 25
   List of Breeders and Rescue Websites 27
   Legal Requirements and Dog Licensing 31
      United States Licensing for Dogs 32
      United Kingdom Licensing for Dogs 33

- How Much Should I Need? 34
- Are You Financially Prepared? 34

Chapter Three: The Ultimate Great Dane Health and Medical Guide 44

- Common Health Problems 45
- **Gastric Torsion** 62
- **Heart Disease** 62
- **Cancer** 63
- **Wobbler's Syndrome** 63
- **Hypothyroidism** 64
- **Arthritis** 64
- Recommended Vaccinations 64
- Vaccination Tips 74

Chapter Four: Fact or Bluff? What to Believe? 76

- Fun Great Dane Facts 77
- Myths Surrounding the Great Dane 85

Chapter Five: What Will My Great Dane Eat? A Primer 90

- The Nutritional Needs of Dogs 91
- How to Select a Healthy Dog Food Brand 95
- Tips for Feeding Your Pet 102
- Toxic Foods to Avoid 103

Chapter Six: Breeding Your Great Dane 106

Basic Dog Breeding Information 107

Mating Behavior of Dogs 108

Tips for Breeding Your Great Dane 110

The Labor Process of Your Great Dane 111

Chapter Seven: The Great Dane's Ultimate Cheat Sheet ... 114

Basic Great Dane Information 115

Habitat Requirements 116

Nutritional Needs 117

Breeding Information 118

Photo Credits 120

References 121

Introduction

There are over 340 dog breeds in the whole world, choosing the one for you might be really overwhelming. People only know the common dog breeds, especially the small ones. One of the 'forgotten' breeds is the Great Dane,

Great Danes is truly one of the majestic breeds in the dog world. They are large yet gentle breed - truly fitting its name 'the gentle giants'. Further, these dogs are called the "Apollo of dogs," because they are compared to Apollo, the Greek sun god, which is the highest thing in the sky. With its great stature, the Great Dane is truly the Apollo of dogs, but behind its bulky features, the Danes are one of the sweetest and affectionate dogs that you will ever meet. A plus is that this breed likes to play and care for children.

Introduction

When the time comes and you decide to take care of a Great Dane, you need to take note of these things, as they are essential in keeping you and your dog happy.

This breed does not really go well with small spaces, not only because of its size but also for their high energy and need for plenty of exercise. Other than that, if this is the first time you will take care of a Great Dane - you might need to find a mentor who will help you to train your pup.

The traits above might scare you, what might entice you is that this breed is sensitive to orders, which means it is easy to train and easy going. Due to its short fur, this breed is not really suited for cold weather but can stand mid to high temperatures. An advantage to it is that your pet requires minimal grooming and very easy to groom but they may shed a lot.

Further, this breed will surely befriend anyone in your family, whether it is dogs, strangers, or even your friends' dog! It can get along with big or small dogs.

You do not need to worry as this breed does not easily gain weight because they are very active and wants to play around. This breed needs to be regularly exercised as they have high energy levels and are pretty playful.

Introduction

You need to have a lot of guts to take care of this lovable and playful creature. Aside from that, you need to allot a lot of time and effort to make your pet really happy. With this book, you will gain essential information that will make your journey with your pet a breeze. Make sure you go through every part thoroughly so you will not miss anything! Have fun reading.

Introduction

Chapter One: Let's Start With the Basics

The real ancestors of the Great Dane are still not known, but their close relatives have existed for a long time.

Historians have found drawings of dog in Egyptian monuments dating back to 3000 B.C. which greatly resembles the breed. Further, Chinese writers have written descriptions of dogs in 1121 B.C. It is believed that the Great Dane is a mix of the English Mastiff and Irish Wolfhound.

The Great Dane that we have now is more mature and peaceful in nature, unlike the original which was primarily bred for hunting wild European boars. They have power, tenacity, intelligence which is perfectly fit for the task as hunters.

Chapter One: Let's Start with the Basics

The noblemen in Germany were astounded with this breed that they began to make them as their body guards, especially for their big estates.

In 1592, 600 packs of Great Danes were brought by the Duke of Braunschweig to hunt boars, it was reported that all of them were males. Germany declared the Great Dane as their national dog in 1876. Some groups called the breed as "Deutsche dogge".

The Great Dane were introduced in the United States of America in the mid-1800s.

In 1887, the American Kennel Club recognized the Great Dane as a part of their club. Later, in 1889, the Great Mastiff Club of America was founded but later renamed to the Great Dane Club of America.

General Appearance and Showmanship Qualities

The Great Dane can be described as dignified, strong, and elegant. It is a large breed that has a well-formed, smooth, and powerful body. Further, we can describe the Great Dane as courageous, confident, never clumsy, and spirited.

Chapter One: Let's Start with the Basics

Here are the other standards that the American Kennel Club has set for a good breed of a Great Dane:

Head – A Great Dane's head is rectangular, distinguished, long, finely chiselled, and expressive especially under their eyes. When you look at them from their sides, the dog's forehead must have a sharp set off starting from the nose bridge (also called as a stop). The plane of the muzzle and the skull must parallel and straight to one another. The female's head is more finely formed, while the male has a pronounced masculinity in it.

BODY

The body of the Great Dane has distinguished features that you need to look out for.

Neck - The dog's neck should be high set, long, well arched, muscular but still firm. When starting from the nape, you can see a smooth yet gradual flow into their withers. The underline of the neck should be clean. There should not be a pronounced sternum but the fore chest must be well developed.

Chapter One: Let's Start with the Basics

Forequarters - When viewed from the side, the forequarters must be muscular and strong. The Great Dane should have a strong, ring angled shoulder blades that is well articulated with its upper arm. The upper tip of the shoulder and the elbow joint should be perpendicular to one another. There must be a well - developed, securely attached, and firm hold of the ligaments, muscles, shoulder blades, and rib cage. The upper arm and shoulder blade needs to be the same length. There must be a slight slope in its strong pasterns. It is noticeable that the Great Dane's feet are rounded and compacted with well-arched toes; no toes should be peeping out. Their nails must be strong, short, and very dark.

Coat - The Great Dane's coat should be thick, clean, and short. It has a glossy appearance.

Eyes - A Great Dane, typically, has medium size, dark, deep set yet a lively and intelligent expression. They have relatively tight yet almond-shaped eyelids with well - developed brows. In the harlequin variety of Great Danes, the eyes should be dark. Light to different colored eyes is not really desirable.

Ears - The ears should be medium in size, moderately thick, high set yet folded near the cheek. The top line of the ear

Chapter One: Let's Start with the Basics

should be well - levelled with the skull. Some dogs have cropped ear, but remember that those ears should be proportionate to the head and ear size. The nose should be black, all other colors are undesirable.

Hindquarters - The Great Dane's hindquarters should be muscular, well angulated, broad, and strong. The hock joins must be perfectly straight, especially when viewed from the rear. Its feet must be compact and round.

Colors, Markings, and Patterns

There are different variations of a Great Dane, such as: Mantle, Black, Fawn, Brindle, Blue, and Harlequin. Each type has its distinctive feature that sets them apart.

Mantle - the color must be white and black, further, it has a solid black blank all over its body. It has a white muzzle on its black skull.

Black - The overall color must be a glossy black. Any other markings are undesirable.

Chapter One: Let's Start with the Basics

Fawn - In this variation, the color must be yellow gold with a black mask. The black markings should be appeared on the eyebrows and eye rims.

Brindle - The overall base color should be yellow gold with strong black cross stripes. It is preferable that it has black mask.

Blue - The body color must be pure steel blue. Any other colors are undesirable.

Harlequin - The dominant color must be pure white with patches of irregular black shapes. These patches must be well distributed throughout its body.

Gait - The Great Dane's gait is strong and powerful. No rolling, bouncing, or even tossing of both the top line and its body. The backline must be levelled and parallel to the ground.

Chapter One: Let's Start with the Basics

Height

Generally, male Great Dane stands at 32-36 inches (81.28 - 91.44 cm) while females stand at 29 - 33 inches (73.66 cm - 83.82 cm). The Great Dane is also called the gentle giant due to its size. Although it is known that they stand very tall, first time owners somehow don't expect the growth rate of their dogs. Below is a guide on the growth rate of your Great Dane:

Age	Height in Inches
At Birth to Six Weeks	No data available
Two Months	13 in - 18 in
Three Months	17 in - 23 in
Fourth Months	21 in - 26 in
Five Months	23 in - 30 in
Six Months	26 in - 33 in
Seven Months	27 in - 34 in
Eight Months	27 in - 34 in
Nine Months	27 in - 35 in
One Year	29 in - 36 in
Adult	28 in - 38 in

Chapter One: Let's Start with the Basics

Note that the given data is just a close estimate. There are variation for your dog due to its diet and other restriction.

Weight

The male weighs 54 - 90 kg (119.05 pounds - 198.416 pounds), while the female weighs 45 - 59 kg (99.208 pounds - 130.073 pounds)

Lifespan

Typically, a Great Dane lives between 8 to 10 years. Some even only live for 6 or 7 years, and only a few reaches to 12. It is quite ironic that a great big dog lives only for a few years. Scientists have tirelessly researched on this condition, but they did note that bigger dogs age faster than smaller ones.

Diet and Feeding

A common misconception of the Great Dane owners is that they need to overfeed their dogs due to its big size. They want their dogs to be bigger as soon as possible.

Chapter One: Let's Start with the Basics

We need to let the dogs grow in their natural pace. If we keep feeding your Great Dane so much, it could result to grave health issues such as weight and joint problems. We must follow a strict feeding schedule and a regulated food quantity. Great Danes are severely prone to bone problems due to its stature. In this scenario, the diet must be low in protein and fat, while the calcium is apt.

Other than that, the food bowl of your Great Dane must not be on the floor, but instead, keep it elevated. There are special food bowls so your dogs will have easy access to it.

Feeding Your Puppy

Food is essential for your puppy. Your Great Dane steadily grows from the 12 to 18 months. During this stage, you need to frequently change the schedule and amount on a monthly basis. During the first six months, you need to feed it three times a day. Below is a chart on the feeding amount for your puppy:

Chapter One: Let's Start with the Basics

Age	Amount
Two months	Two to four cups
Six months	Six to eight cups
Seven to nine months	Two meals a day

You should feed the last meal for the day at least two hours before it sleep. Also, increase the food intake to seven to ten cups from its nine months up to a year old.

Feeding an Adult Dog

Adult dogs should be fed twice a day. Males can be given eight to fourteen cups, while females should be given six to nine cups. You can give more if your dog is quite active, gets a lot of exercise, and highly energetic.

Below are some feeding essentials that you need to remember for your dog:

- ✓ Don't feed growth formula or puppy food to avoid accelerated growth. This may lead to bone and joint problem.
- ✓ The food should contain 12%-20% fat and 25% protein.

Chapter One: Let's Start with the Basics

- ✓ Do not free feed your Great Dane
- ✓ Do not give table food to them.
- ✓ Strictly follow a feeding schedule to avoid over and underfeeding.
- ✓ Let the dog rest for up to 90 minutes before play time.
- ✓ Have elevated feeders to prevent digestive problems.

Health

Just like any other dogs, Great Danes are susceptible to various illnesses such as: bloat, cardiomyopathy, or even cancer. Other than that, Great Danes can develop Wobbler's syndrome, hip dysplasia, or even hereditary cataracts. Remember that some of the diseases may be inherited from their parents, or from the way your raise them up. So take great care and precaution of your dog.

We will discuss in detail some other illnesses on the succeeding chapters.

Chapter One: Let's Start with the Basics

Personality and Temperament

According to the American Kennel Club, a Great Dane must be never timid, spirited, dependable, courageous, and friendly. These, together with its physical characteristics, create a great personality for your Great Dane.

A proper Great Dane can be made into a trusted, affectionate, loving, trusting, and outstanding family companion. You should train your Dane not to be overly protective and aggressive to avoid any incidents. You need to be in control of your Great Dane no matter what, to be able to keep them as gentle as possible.

Your Great Dane needs moderate exercise and doesn't want to be cramped up into small spaces. It needs to have a constant companion because it doesn't do great when left alone. You need to constantly train and walk your dog as much as possible to build its confidence and create a great temperament.

You need to properly train your dog on obedience as they tend to get bossy due to its size. But take note, Great Danes are sensitive, so you need to train them using cheerful tactics. They might be confused with your techniques and make them distrust you even more.

Chapter One: Let's Start with the Basics

If You Want...

- an elegant and big mastiff-type dog.
- easy-care coat that comes in many color
- mild - mannered and easy going
- only needs moderate exercise
- imposing yet not aggressive with other people

If You Do Not Want...

- a huge dog that will surely take a lot of space
- a large and heavy dog that will surely sit at your lap and put its weight against your leg
- playful, especially during its puppyhood
- has separation anxiety when left too long
- can be too aggressive or fearful if not socialized enough
- strong willed due to its size
- always drooling
- can have serious health problems and short life
- have serious legal liabilities

Chapter One: Let's Start with the Basics

Quick Facts

In this part, we will give you a quick rundown on the essential information about your pet the Great Dane. These information can serve as your 'cheat' sheet in the future.

Origin: Germany

Pedigree: people consider the breed as a crossbreed Irish Wolfhound and English Mastiff

Breed Size: big size (working group)

Body Type and Appearance: Has a big, bulky body. It stands tall and alert for intruders.

Group: American Kennel Club, Westminster Kennel Club, Great Dane Club of America

Height: 76-68 cm (male) and 71-81 cm (female)

Weight: 54-90 kg (male) and 45-59 kg (female)

Coat Length: short-hair

Coat Texture: glossy

Color: brindle, fawn, black, harlequin, blue, and mantle

Temperament: devoted, reserved, gentle, confident, loving, friendly

Chapter One: Let's Start with the Basics

Strangers: friendly around strangers

Other Dogs: both genders get along with other dogs

Other Pets: gets along well with other pets

Training: due to its size, you need to establish authority over your Great Dane

Exercise Needs: needs 30 to 60 minutes of daily exercise.

Health Conditions: generally healthy but can contract common illnesses such as Canine hip dysplasia, Pattelar, ear infection, and others

Lifespan: average 8 - 10 years.

These are just essential information that you need to know about your Great Dane. Now you are armed with the basic knowledge, you can continue your journey into knowing your Great Dane more.

Chapter One: Let's Start with the Basics

Chapter Two: Taking Care of Your Great Dane

After reading the first chapter, we are very sure that you are now well-equipped with essential knowledge about our gentle giant. Why not continue the journey into knowing our lovable pet? Great Danes are the gentle giants of the dog world. They are your affectionate yet huge dogs that would love a play time whenever it can. If you think you can handle this kind of behaviour, then you need to purchase this breed immediately! In this part, we will discuss more essential information about our beloved pet, such as purchasing your dog legally and costings. You need to read this information as they are vital to keep you on track, especially with a budget.

Chapter Two: Taking Care of Your Great Dane

What Makes It a Great Pet

Buying a house pet is big decision. You need to be, not only mentally prepared but also financially prepared. If you ready yourself in these circumstances, you might as well be in danger with overspending and be under prepared.

Great Danes are lovable creatures, although they might need more training than usual. Since they are big pets, they might be bossy and overpower novice owners. They loved to be walked and regularly exercised to learn new tricks and be tame. You can also create a guard dog out of this pet. Just make sure that your pet will not be overprotective as they may also get overly aggressive at some point.

Where to Purchase your Great Dane

You have a lot of options on where you can buy your very first puppy. In this section, we will be listing down places, as well as its pros and cons. Read on to know which option is the best for you. Buying a pet is a tedious and difficult task. It will require you to devote a lot of time and effort to know where and who to buy your pet from. A great breeder would give you a lot of information about your dog's history as well as sell it for a cheap price.

Chapter Two: Taking Care of Your Great Dane

Buying a dog will be an exhausting process; you will be calling and going to places to find the best dog possible.

Local Pet Stores

Local pet stores are one of the popular choices when buying pets. A reason for this choice is that pet stores are easily accessible to many people. Other than that, some pet stores may even deliver your puppy if you live near the store. Unfortunately, most pet shops will not give you enough details of your puppy and its history. Also, some stores will not take good care of their puppies because they have too many dogs to handle at one time.

This is a good option if you have no time in finding your dog. You will just go to a local shop and pick out the Great Dane for you. However, if you want to choose the best among rest, you might need to look for another path. You need to have great determination to find the best pet for you.

Backyard/Private Breeders

Private breeders are one of the best alternates in finding your puppy. A good referral will greatly help your decision.

Chapter Two: Taking Care of Your Great Dane

A reason for this choice is you can truly get to know the breeder, the puppy, and the parents. The breeder could give you all of the information needed about the pup that they are selling. Also, you can settle the price and the breeder may even share some techniques on taking care of the pup.

However, a disadvantage for this option is that you need to comb through houses after houses and personally visit and inspect the puppies. You need time, money, and a mode of transportation to go back and forth to different places and get your dream pup.

This option is for those who like to talk and meet new breeders. If you want to take this road, you could potentially set up a network of dog owners and friendship. However, this option is not for people who are very busy and do not want to socialize with other people.

Online Stores

When the internet has become a popular a poplar shopping place for people, many people opt to buy from online sellers rather than go to physical shops. This option is truly for the busy person because you can look and meet for the purchase. You can even join forums to know the characteristics of a great breed.

Chapter Two: Taking Care of Your Great Dane

Unfortunately, you can't thoroughly critique the breed, background, and health issues of the puppy. You just need to take know of its physical characteristics and truly know if the breed is great or not.

This is a difficult path to go through. You need to gather a lot of information before buying from online sellers. You need to be on the lookout for scamming activities, you need to thoroughly research on the breeder, know and understand if he truly has a background idea and experience in breeding Great Dane. You can also ask essential questions about the parents and the puppy. Other than that, make sure you know the signs of a great breed.

Great sellers will not keep secrets about its pup. You should not trust a seller who will withhold information, especially about the parents' history and medical information.

After reading this section, you now have an idea on where to buy your Great Dane puppy. Make sure you have thoroughly thought of your choice before moving forward.

Tell Tale Signs of a Reputable Breeder

After knowing where to buy your pet, you need to buy WHO to buy the breed from. We do not want you buy an unhealthy puppy that you will be stuck for 8 to 10 years.

Chapter Two: Taking Care of Your Great Dane

You need to devote time and effort in finding a great breeder that will answer all your queries about your pets, take note of these things before going out and buy your first pet. Below down are all the information as well as its pros and cons so you will not regret your decision after a while.

Here are some signs that you have a great Great Dane breeder:

- Ask help from your friends and family. A good recommendation is needed to find a great breeder.
- Join online forums and get to know breeders from your area.
- Find local dog owners and ask them about their opinions on the breeder of your choice.
- Research! Great Dane website provides some information about great breeders.
- Make sure that you fact-check the website to truly know that you can trust what is written there, especially the part about the breeders.
- If the website lacks the information that you need about the breeders or the facilities, change your option immediately as you are clearly wasting your time,

Chapter Two: Taking Care of Your Great Dane

- Contact each person immediately. You need to ask them probing information that will let you see if the breeders are legitimate or not.
- Remove breeders who can't your questions honestly and truthfully, this will eliminate breeders that are incapable of giving you the information that you need.
- Just like you, a reputable breeder will ask questions about yourself. A great breeder would want a safe and happy home for its dogs.
- Comb through every detail, although difficult, will yield the best result possible.
- You need to personally visit the breeders and ask them to tour you to their facilities.
- Eliminate places that are dirty and unorganized. You need to safeguard your pup against bacteria and viruses.
- If you can't still make up your mind, go back and go through the list again.
- If you have chosen a great breeder, contact them immediately and reserve your chosen pup.

Chapter Two: Taking Care of Your Great Dane

Characteristics of a Healthy Breed

You, now, need to get to know your future pup because you already know where to buy the pup and who to buy it from. You need to look for a Great Dane that is not only well rounded physically, behaviourally, and mentally.

Just like the other choices, you need to allot time to get to know your puppy. You need to make sure that the Great Dane's characteristics truly fits yours, otherwise, you will have a hard time especially in obedience training.

We will list down some great characteristics of a healthy pup. We have thoroughly researched about the qualities of the Great Dane. Check off the item that applies to the pup that you will be buying.

The Great Dane's Physical Characteristics

- Look thoroughly the puppy's body and see if there are any signs of potential injuries and illnesses.
- Make sure that its gums and teeth are also in good condition
- Do not pick Great Danes that are lethargic and can't move because they might be sick.
- Check the Great Dane's coat color and skin.
- The Great Dane's stomach shouldn't be swollen or distended.

Chapter Two: Taking Care of Your Great Dane

- The Great Dane should be able to walk or run properly without difficulty.
- The Great Dane's ears should be clear and clean with no inflammation or discharge.
- The Great Dane should have bright and clear eyes eyes with no brownish discharge.

The Great Dane's Behavior

- The Great Dane needs to be playful and active, interacting with each other in a healthy way.
- You must play with the puppies individually. You can understand their individual traits and select the best on that fits your personality.
- Select the Great Dane pup that is not afraid of human contact. Those who are afraid of human contact are probably not socialized.
- You need to observe the litter as a whole, and watch how the pups interact with one another so you can truly know their personalities.
- If you can see all the puppies are in amazing condition and well socialized, it is a good size that your breeder is truly reputable. You just need to choose the puppy that is truly fitted for you.

Chapter Two: Taking Care of Your Great Dane

Important Note

You can't take in puppies that are less than eight weeks old. Some states do not permit the selling of these puppies. Make sure that the puppies are eating solid food and fully weaned.

If the breeder does not give out this information, observe your puppies to know if they can survive on its own.

List of Breeders and Rescue Websites

After extensively researching your pup, you probably know the characteristics of a Great Dane puppy. Make sure that you fully know all the details before buying, as to not waste not only time but also money.

Aside from the given choices above, there is still an option on where you can get your puppy. This option is for those who are willing to save a life and grant a new beginning for an individual. You can still adopt an abandoned and unloved Great Dane in your area. There is hundreds of Great Dane that needs to be cared for. Adopting a Great Dane will open up new opportunities for it to grow and further flourish. Although it might be difficult to buy and train an adult dog, some stores would give you free accessories and cages.

Chapter Two: Taking Care of Your Great Dane

Aside from that, adult Great Danes will show you love you have never felt before. Aside from this, some dogs are already spayed or neutered, vaccinated, or even house trained. Here are some breeders and adoption rescue sites in the United Kingdom and United States:

United States Breeders and Rescue Websites

San Antonio Great Dane Rescue - Homeward Bound Dog Rescue

<http://texasgreatdane.org/>

Rocky Mountain Great Dane Rescue

<https://rmgreatdane.org/>

Southern Style Great Dane Rescue

<http://southernstylegreatdanerescue.org/>

Save Rocky the Great Rescue and Rehab

<http://www.saverockythegreatdane.org/>

Harlequin Haven Great Dane Rescue

<http://hhdane.com/>

Chapter Two: Taking Care of Your Great Dane

Great Dane Rescue

<http://www.greatdanerescueinc.com/about_us/mission.html>

White Kisses Great Dane Rescue

<https://www.whitekissesgreatdanerescue.com/>

Dane Outreach

<http://www.daneoutreach.org/>

Dane Heaven, Inc.

<https://www.danehaveninc.com/>

Upper Midwest Great Dane Rescue

<https://thegreatdanerescue.com/our-dogs/available-dogs/>

Waters Edge Great Dane Rescue, Inc.

<http://www.watersedgegreatdanerescue.com/>

The Mid-Atlantic Great Dane Rescue League

<http://www.magdrl.org/>

Ozr Great Dane Rescue Inc.

<https://www.ozrgreatdanerescue.org/>

Northwest Florida Great Dane Rescue

<http://www.nwflgdr.com/>

Chapter Two: Taking Care of Your Great Dane

North Mississippi Great Dane Rescue
<http://northmissgreatdanes.com/>

United Kingdom Breeders and Rescue Websites

The Great Dane Adoption Society
<http://www.danes.org.uk/>

Daneline International Charitable Foundation
<https://www.daneline.co.uk/>

TJ Danes Rescue
<http://tjdanesrescues.org.uk/>

National Great Dane Rescue
<http://www.ngdr.co.uk/>

Great Danes Owners Forum
<http://www.greatdaneowners.co.uk/index.php?/forum/28-great-dane-rescue-and-re-homing/>

Great Dane Rescue of New England
<http://www.gdrne.org/>

Great Dane Care Charitable Trust
<http://www.great-dane-care.org.uk/>

Great Dane Rescue
<http://www.greatdanerescueinc.com/events/international_resuces.html>

South Western Great Dane Club
<http://www.swgdc.co.uk/index.asp?pageid=630129>

Midland and West of England Great Dane
<http://www.midlandandwestgdc.org.uk/links.html>

Great Dane Angels
<https://www.greatdaneangels.org/needs-a-home/>

The Northern Great Dane Club
<http://www.thenortherngreatdaneclub.com/>

Legal Requirements and Dog Licensing

If you are eager to buy your own Great Dane as your house pet, there are rules and regulations that you need to be well versed of. Licensing of pets vary from origin, regions, or even states.

Chapter Two: Taking Care of Your Great Dane

In the United States there are no federal requirements for licensing dogs or even cats – these rules are regulated at the state level. While it is true that most states do not have a mandatory requirement for people to license their dogs, it is always a good idea to do so because it will not only serve as protection for your pet but also for you.

Here are some further information that you need to know about licensing and registering your pet Great Dane in both United States and Great Britain.

United States Licensing for Dogs

There is no existing federal requirement for licensing your pet Great Dane in the United States, each state might have different licensing requirements that you need to look out for. Most states require dog owners to register and license their pet dogs.

How to Obtain a License?

You need to have a proof that your pet has been recently vaccinated against rabies. This proof needs to be renewed each year. Dog licenses are only $25 (£16.25) per year, which is not really expensive. There might be additional things to bring when registering to different states. The license given to you is temporary until you have

Chapter Two: Taking Care of Your Great Dane

submitted the necessary documents to the proper authorities.

Even if your region does not require a registering and licensing your dog, it is a pretty good measure to do so. If, in an unfortunate accident, your dog gets lost, having a proper identification will help you to locate it easier. Your dog's license has an identification number which is linked to you, which provides contact details for easy rescue of your dog. Further, you can add contact information on your dog's collar and leash for added security.

United Kingdom Licensing for Dogs

Unlike the United States, the United Kingdom strictly requires dog owners to license their dogs.

The main difference, however, is that your dog does not need an initial vaccination because the disease has already been eradicated. You need to renew your dog annually and is fairly cheap. You might need to secure several permits when you want to travel with your pet, especially internationally.

Chapter Two: Taking Care of Your Great Dane

How Much Should I Need?

In this section, we will be tackling in detail how much you need to have in order to raise your Great Dane. We will give you every expense you might encounter. Here, we will discuss purchase fees, accessories, toys, licensing grooming supplies, and other related needs.

Are You Financially Prepared?

Purchasing a new pet is a big deal. You need to be holistically prepared in this endeavour. You must prepare not only your mind and soul, but also your pockets for the upcoming expenses. Adding a new member in the family means more treats, grooming, food, toys, and other necessities. You need to make sure that you have enough to raise your dog without blowing your budget.

Having a dog is just like raising your own child, you need to list down every expenditure that you will come across to adjust your budget accordingly. At first, this might be difficult, but you will get a hang of it after some time.

The total cost for your Great Dane expenses will heavily depend on the kind and availability of resources in your area. Some stores might grab the opportunity to raise the prices if they have limited stocks and no real competition

Chapter Two: Taking Care of Your Great Dane

around the area. Other than that, the quality and brand will help you know how much you need to spend and how long you can use the item up.

Here, we will give you an insight if you are truly financially prepared in purchasing and taking care of your own Great Dane.

Price of a Great Dane

Great Danes are majestic. They stand tall and guard their humans and properties against enemies. Other than that, they can be your cuddly pets who surely love to walk, run, and even have obedience training often. This is one of the reasons why people love to take care and breed Great Danes.

You have different options on where to get your Great Dane. You can either adopt or purchase your own dog. Adopting a dog is a cheaper option, but remembers that it is much more difficult to take care of an adopted dog rather than a newborn one. On the succeeding chapters, we will talk about the difference between the two.

Purchasing a Great Dane varies from $400 - $3000. The price seriously depends on the breeder and the dog itself. If the dog can be classified as a show dog, passing the standards of the American Kennel Club, it can be much pricier.

Chapter Two: Taking Care of Your Great Dane

You need to take great precaution in purchasing your Great Dane puppy; you need to remember that even though they are priced high - you can never be too sure about its quality. You need to look at its medical records, the parents' background before purchasing it.

Buying from a trusted friend will mean less cost, while buying from a trusted pet store can mean a greater quality of dog.

Other Essentials

Purchasing your Great Dane puppy is only the initial expense that you will have in the series of expenditure. You need to know that there are a lot more expenses coming up, such as bed, vet consultations, grooming tools, vaccinations, and etc. Although you might not think that they are essential at first, you need to be financially prepared in buying all of these things - as they will come in handy in the near future. These things will make your Great Dane's and your life a breeze. Read on to know more about these things!

Bed ($10-$50)

The Great Dane is known as the gentle giant, with its name, you can surely know that it is big. You need to buy a big bed from the very start because your pet will surely use it for a long time.

Chapter Two: Taking Care of Your Great Dane

Do not be fooled into buying a small sized bed, thinking that you just bought a puppy, remember that your Great Dane grows fast and big.

You need to find a great dog bed that will support your dog's hip. Remember, your Great Dane is susceptible to hip dysplasia. Other than that, find a bed that has comfortable mattress.

Although there are a lot of online shops available right now, it is still best to buy your dog bed in a physical shop. This is vital because you can touch and feel the mattress and see if it fits the needs of your beloved dog. Also, you can choose different structures and designs for your beloved pet. Make sure you buy the best bed that would fit the personality of your beloved pet.

Toys ($20-$100)

You have a lot of toy options for your Great Dane. You need to find the best one for your dearest pet. You can choose from big or small balls, squeaky toys, bones, and etc. Different toys will provide different activities for your dog. This will exercise its body and creativity overtime.

You need to maximize your dog's toys. Use these things for them to learn new tricks and words. Your Great Dane is a highly active dog; it needs constant play time and running around the yard. These toys will help your dog use

Chapter Two: Taking Care of Your Great Dane

his time effectively, especially when left at home.

But, do not just buy and buy toys whenever you can. Teach your dog to use its toys efficiently. Further, you need to teach your dog where to put its toys after playtime. Have a box where your pup can put all of its toys. This will also ensure that you know where all the toys are.

Grooming Tools ($100-$500)

Great Danes are known for its short yet glossy fur. Although this might be a big advantage for you, you should still buy grooming tools for your pet. You need to get essential brushes as well as additional brushes for your furry friend.

There are a big number of brushes for you to choose from. It is best consult your vet and groomer about the necessary tools. Buy these things immediately so you can do the emergency cutting and styling at home.

Also, owning these tools will help you practice grooming your Great Dane. If you learn to groom your own dog, you can save up tons of money by not going to the groomer.

Chapter Two: Taking Care of Your Great Dane

Dog Food and Treats ($50-100)

A healthy dog is a happy dog. In order to keep your dog happy and healthy, you need to provide it with healthy food and treats. Dog food contains nutrients that help your dog to grow and be healthy in the future. You need to feed your dog the dog food in the latter part of its life, as your dog needs special food especially during its puppyhood.

Dog treats are not only used as 'treats' for your dog. You can also use it to train your dog into learning new commands and words for further obedience training.

Buying healthy dog food is essential to promote great health for your dog. This is a vital key for your dog to have the best nutrients. Make sure you study the nutritional value and packaging for you to know everything about the product.

Medical Expenses

There are a lot of medical expenses that you will have when you purchase a pet, it includes the following:

- micro-chipping
- spay/neuter surgery
- vet consultation
- vaccinations

Chapter Two: Taking Care of Your Great Dane

You might think these are only incidental expenses, but you need to save immediately, especially you do not know when you need to rush your pup to the hospital. Further, the other medical expenses are necessary to have a healthy and happy dog in your house.

Micro - chipping

Micro-chipping is not needed by the United States and United Kingdom government. Although this is the scenario, microchipping is an essential step if you want to keep your dog safe.

Your dog might go out unsupervised and might wander off alone. It is best to always track your dog wherever it goes. If this unfortunate event has happened, your dog might be taken into a shelter when it is found wandering alone on the streets, a microchip would be very helpful in identifying your dog and your contact information.

Micro-chipping is a process where a special chip is put under your dog's skin that will carry essential information about the owner. It is a painless procedure that will only cost $50, but can go higher for some states.

Chapter Two: Taking Care of Your Great Dane

Initial Vaccinations

Initial vaccinations are essential to a puppy's life, especially if you have purchased or got your Great Dane at an early age.

You need to give your puppies boosters and vaccines because they are more prone to viral infections, but make sure that your puppy is ready for the vaccination. The mother can give the needed antibodies during its puppyhood stage, but this is not enough to combat all the viruses, illnesses, and diseases in the outside world.

Remember to have your puppies vaccinated; this will definitely lengthen their lifespan. The price of a vaccine starts at $50 but may go up due to different boosters needed by your dog.

Spay/Neuter Surgery

Spay/neuter surgery is one of the hardest but needed decision you need to do for your dog.

If you don't want to breed Great Dane or cannot allot the necessary time to take care of more puppies, this might be the track for you. You might want to consider spaying or neutering because of its benefits. First, spaying/neutering will lessen the chance of uterine infections, breast cancer, and testicular cancer. Also, spaying/neutering will eliminate unwanted puppies from your house.

Chapter Two: Taking Care of Your Great Dane

Further, you male dog won't roam around and find a mate, since it can't go into heat. The price for this surgery depends on the gender of your dog and where you will have it done.

Veterinary Consultations

Visiting a vet is a must for your pet. You should keep your vet on track on the condition of your pet. In turn, your vet will help you take care of your Great Dane and keep it healthy for a long time.

Great Danes needs to have a regular check up every six months. A regular vet check-up is needed if your pet is still a puppy, your vet need to be updated with your puppy's growth and coping mechanism. The average cost of a vet's visit is around $40. It might be pricey at first, but we need to remember that prevention is better than cure. We need to stop the diseases before it even spreads.

Now, you are equipped with essential information that will help you raise your own Great Dane. If you think you can keep up with the budget, now that you know all the expenses that accompany it, you can move forward with your decision. You need to know that these costs are only estimates, but the things are essential to provide a healthy and happy life for you and for your Great Dane.

Chapter Two: Taking Care of Your Great Dane

Chapter Three: The Ultimate Great Dane Health and Medical Guide

Taking care of a dog is just like taking care of your own child. You will start with raising it, knowing the ins and outs of every possibility. Other than that, you need to know the quick hacks or easy remedies to solve easy issues at the comfort of your own home.

You need to be well versed of all the disorders and disorders that may cause future health and medical problems to your Great Dane. The knowledge of the following will help you addressing it quickly and responsibly.

Chapter Three: The Ultimate Great Dane Health Guide

It might be a long shot, but you need to keep an eye on all the signs, symptoms, or causes that may appear to your Great Dane so you can stop everything immediately.

Common Health Problems

In this section, we will provide you with important information that may affect your Great Dane's health. Knowing all of these things will give you basic knowledge on all the things that might happen.

You need to always be careful with your Great Dane's health - especially its weight. Due to its large size, you need to watch how much you feed your Great Dane as they may get easily overweight. Other than that, they may develop several bone diseases due to its weight. Other than that, there are still several diseases to look out for.

Below, you can find the diseases and disorders that may affect your Great Dane.

Home Remedies

Just like small kids, some illnesses are easily taken care of. You should not always panic when there is something wrong with your beloved.

Chapter Three: The Ultimate Great Dane Health Guide

Here, we will be listing down some common health problems your Great Dane might face and how to treat it easily:

1. Ear Infections

The ear infection is one of the most common illnesses for dogs. This infection affects the apartment and backyard dog, big or even small ones. Some causes are: yeast, ear canal hair growth, colds, allergies, bacteria, mites, and etc.

Symptoms include:

- Vulnerability and crying at ear touch
- Vigorous ear scratching
- Crying
- Redness of the ear canal
- Head shaking
- Swelling of the outer areas of the ear

If you notice that your dog is showing even of these symptoms, you can suspect that your dog has an ear infection.

Chapter Three: The Ultimate Great Dane Health Guide

An easy cure is using a cotton ball (but NOT a Q-tip) and a gentle non-alcoholic cleansing solution that would thoroughly clean the ear. Although it is easily preventable, you should still go to your vet to fully assess the situation to fully cure it.

2. Digestive Problems Including Diarrhea and Vomiting

While vomiting or diarrhea should not really bother you, if this will be recurrent - you should be quite alarmed. If your dog vomits or has a lot of diarrhea episodes for more than a day, also look for these other symptoms:

× Presence of blood in the vomit or stool

× Fever

× Loss of appetite

× Black or dark diarrhea

× Crying of pain

× Lethargy

Improper food, allergies, swallowed objects, bacterial infections, pancreatitis, food poisoning, or others are some of the causes of gastrointestinal disease.

Chapter Three: The Ultimate Great Dane Health Guide

Before rushing to your vet, try the following remedies:

- Give the dog plenty of water to combat dehydration
- Give your dog a suspension of water and PeptoBismol
- A spoonful of yogurt will help with the intestinal flora balance.
- Provide the dog rice water to drink. You need toboil one cup of white rice in water, rinse and let the liquid cool, then give it to your dog.

3. Skin Tags

Skin tags are both terrifying for both pets and people. For dog, skin tags are usually benign, but you should still focus on this issue. Skin tags in dogs are quite common and the causes are still under research. Some of the reasons of skin tags are Parasites, genetics, improper skin care, the environment, or a poor diet. However, these skin tags won't make your dog suffer or are not that painful. You should not really fear that skin tags are cancerous. There are several home remedies for this condition and you could try it without much worry.

Chapter Three: The Ultimate Great Dane Health Guide

If you can see that your dog is in pain and looks like a diseases, take your dog immediately to the vet.

4. All Kinds of Worms

Parasites and dogs are arch enemies; however, all dogs will suffer from this problem at least once in their lives. There is several kinds of worms that dogs will come in contact to, and some of them (hookworms) will be fatal in puppies.

The symptoms for worm infestations are the following:

- Scooting on its bottom
- Loss of appetite
- Weight loss
- Dryness of the coat
- Lethargy / or unexplained agitation
- Diarrhea
- Vomiting

Chapter Three: The Ultimate Great Dane Health Guide

You should not really treat the worms on your own. Some medicine may kill some worms but will not kill them all. However, some remedies may soothe the pain until you take them to the vet.

- If your dog likes some garlic in the food. You can mix a crushed garlic clove in the food

- Chop some pumpkin seeds in its food bowl

- Add raw chopped or grated carrots in the food bowl

5. Allergic Dermatitis

If your pet's skin is flaky, itching, irritated, too dry, too oily, has hair loss patches, or even red in color, your dog could have allergic dermatitis. Some factors include: infections, hormonal imbalance, allergies, or even parasites. Bring your dog immediately to the vet so he can diagnose the cause and give the correct treatment.

You could also control the skin condition through proper nutrition. Remember to give your dog good quantities of anti-oxidants, essential fatty acids, and proteins. Also, do not neglect preventative method against ticks or fleas.

Chapter Three: The Ultimate Great Dane Health Guide

6. Dental Diseases

By now, you must know that dental diseases also exist in dogs. You can easily prevent it by giving rawhide chews, teeth-cleaning toys and products. The disease could also be linked to heart disease, kidney problems, diabetes and so much more. Better start caring for it, before it gets worse.

Common symptoms include:

- Smelly breath
- Pain
- Eating and chewing difficulties
- Head shaking
- Swollen face

Only a specialist should treat the disease. However, you can also try brushing your dog's teeth using the recommended dog toothpaste. Further you can feed your dog's raw carrots, chewable toys and boys that contain cleaning property.

Chapter Three: The Ultimate Great Dane Health Guide

7. Urinary Tract Infections

Diet is one of the reasons why Urinary Tract Infection exists in the dog world. Other causes are the following: fungal infection, bacteria, immune infections, or bladder stones.

Common symptoms of UTI are the following:

- Fever
- Backache
- Frequent urination
- Lethargy
- Blood in the urine
- Urination straining

You should immediately consult your vet on what antibiotics and treatment your dog will undergo. An initial step would be regulating and lowering your dog's protein, phosphorus, calcium, and magnesium intake. Other than that, you could also feed it with Ulva Ursi leaf, blueberries, marshmallow roots, vegetables, raw fruits, yogurt, parsley leaves, and juniper berries. Combine these foods with vitamin B supplements, and it will slowly heal your pet.

Chapter Three: The Ultimate Great Dane Health Guide

8. Liver Diseases

You should really worry if something is wrong with your dog's liver. There are several causes of liver diseases, such as: poor nutrition, toxic substances, viral and bacterial infection that your dog may have eaten. Also, genetics and the environment could contribute to the disease.

The following are the symptoms of liver disease:

- Jaundice
- Sudden weight and appetite loss
- Extreme lethargy or depression
- Pale gums
- Build-up of fluid in the abdomen – which should not be mistaken with sudden weight gain
- Dark - colored urine

You should establish a good relationship with your vet to be able to get the correct diagnosis and treatment possible. You could also feed your pet the following:

- liver support natural supplement
- antioxidants, vitamins,
- anti-inflammatory herbs (parsley for instance),
- milk thistle

Chapter Three: The Ultimate Great Dane Health Guide

9. The Flu

Just like humans, your pet could also get the flu. Symptoms include:

- Moist or dry coughs
- Sneezing
- Runny noses
- Fever
- breathing problems
- bloody coughs
- Anorexia
- runny eyes
- and ear infections

You should provide your dog with the following remedies to stop its flue:

- Have plenty of fresh water source
- Don't take your dog out in the park or crowded places
- Introduce garlic in its meal if it likes it

Chapter Three: The Ultimate Great Dane Health Guide

- Add a nutritious diet rich in herbs and vegetables that have antibiotic and anti-inflammatory c properties. Supplement its diet with Vitamin C-rich veggies.

- Keep it in a peaceful and calm, cozy and warm environment

10. Conjunctivitis

Conjunctivitis is a sure headache for a lot of dog owners. Your dog's eye will become pink, itchy, runny or dry, irritated, and swollen. Further, your dog may blink often, accumulate mucus, and shed tears. There will also be a follicle formation in the eye area.

The causes of conjunctivitis are the following: ascribed to bacteria, traumas (foreign bodies), dust environment pollutants, viruses, allergies, immune-mediated diseases, chemicals or medication.

If you suspect there is something in your dog's eye, consider doing the following:

- Use aloe vera and green tea to clean the dog's eyes as well.

- Wash your dog's eyes with cooled chamomile tea and a clean, soft cloth

Chapter Three: The Ultimate Great Dane Health Guide

- clean your dog's eye thoroughly with lukewarm water
- Feed your dog a diet rich in zinc, vitamin C and B.

There are other more common dog illnesses your pup may come in contact during its lifetime. Make sure you monitor their activities regularly to know what is happening and if something is wrong with them. There are initial steps you can do to keep your dog healthy, such as giving them proper hygiene, having peaceful environment, clean living space, and feeding them correctly.

There are also severe diseases that your dog may come across, read on to know more.

Eye diseases

Dry Eyes

This eye disease occurs when a dog has not produced sufficient tears to keep its eyes lubricated. This may result with mucoid discharge that will penetrate one's eye. In this scenario, you might see a big "gunk" around its eyes, your Great Dane's eyelid may rub with the cornea making it very cloudy.

Chapter Three: The Ultimate Great Dane Health Guide

Cherry Eyes

This eye disease happens when there is a prolapse in the third eyelid of your dog. You can see that there is a development of red mass on the corner of the affected eye.

Juvenile Cataract

This usually happens to adult Great Danes or to those who are suffers from diabetes. Your dog would experience and would have 'clouding' in its eye.

Entropion

You can see that your dog will have a gooey eye discharge that could further lead to more serious problem like cataract, corneal ulceration, or glaucoma.

Glaucoma

This disease can change the function and structure of your Great Dane's eyes. The reason for this disease is the change of pressure on your dog's eye. If left untreated, your dog could be blind from this eye disease. Some symptoms that you may notice will include blurring of vision, eye protrusion, and red painful eyes with cloudy corneas.

You need to annually visit your vet for him/her to check the eye pressure of your Great Danes, because they are prone to glaucoma. Your dog will experience much pain and will be blind if left untreated.

Chapter Three: The Ultimate Great Dane Health Guide

This disease typically begins at the age of 3-6 years, and is usually genetic. This can be treated medically to provide comfort for your pet as well as the restoration of the vision of your pet. However, your dog might need surgery in the worst case scenario.

Corneal Wounds

The cornea is skin-like clear tissue that covers the surface of the eye. Just like any other parts of the body, the dog's cornea could be cut, injured, punctured usually the damage is caused by trauma, like when your beloved Great Dane runs through something and its eye gets poked.

In other cases, genetic abnormality is a big factor that could your dog at risk. You can easily assess if your dog has a corneal wound, it would often rub its eye and squint excessively because of the pain, and also you can see that it has excess drainage and reddish in color.

The basic treatment for this disease is using ointments or antibiotic eye drops, so your dog's eye can rest and relieve its pain. In severe cases, further treatments and surgery may be needed to fully heal it.

Chapter Three: The Ultimate Great Dane Health Guide

Pink Eye

The mucus membrane that serves as the covering of the inside of all your dogs' eyelid and some parts of the eyeball is called the conjunctiva.

"Conjunctivitis" or "pink eye" can be interchange but still simply mean "inflammation of the conjunctiva." The symptoms for this disease include swollen and reddened conjunctiva, discomfort, and eye discharge.

Conjunctivitis could be considered as a symptom of disease, not a disease itself. There are various conditions that causes conjunctivitis in dogs, which includes physical irritation (like inward growing eyelashes and dust), allergic reactions, and infections (viral and bacterial are most common). To treat this, you need to know the underlying cause. Sterile saline eye washes are easily available over the counter and can be used to remove irritants from your Great Dane's eyes. These bacterial eye infections can be easily resolved when you treat it with an appropriate prescription antibiotic ointment or eye drop.

There is only a low chance that your dog could catch a pink eye, but you should thoroughly wash your hands before and after applying your dog's eye medication. Make sure that you contact your vet immediately if you have not

Chapter Three: The Ultimate Great Dane Health Guide

resolved the issue after two or three days after self-medication. If you fail to secure a vet's appointment, it could worsen your Great Dane's situation.

Progressive Retinal Atrophy

Some eye diseases in dogs can be difficult to spot. One example is the progressive retinal atrophy (PRA), which causes dogs to slowly become blind even though the eyes appear normal. The PRA's first symptom is often the difficulty seeing things at night. It might progress until your dog's could not see properly and the inability of recognizing things properly. Up to this day, there is no cure for PRA. Fortunately, dogs easily adapt to being blind.

Face diseases/problems

Aside from eye diseases, there are still some face diseases that your dog could have in the future. Here are some of the diseases:

Brachycephalic Syndrome

Easily speaking, this disease blocks the airway of your dog. This causes coughing and gagging, fainting, noisy breathing, collapsing episodes or fatigue especially while exercising.

Chapter Three: The Ultimate Great Dane Health Guide

Cleft Lip/Palate

This usually happens when the roof of the mouth or the opening of the lip didn't process normally during its conception.

Other diseases

Patellar Luxation

This disease is commonly known as arthritis, which can even affect young dogs. It is a painful disease that surely affects the dog's comfort, even emotional well being, and lifestyle.

Hip Dysplasia

It is a common form of arthritis. Hip Dysplasia refers to the abnormality in development and growth of the ball and socket on the Great Dane's hip.

Renal Dysplasia

This disease severely affects puppies. It is a serious developmental disorder affecting your Great Dane's kidney. The underlying cause of this disease is the underdevelopment of one's kidney.

Chapter Three: The Ultimate Great Dane Health Guide

Gastric Torsion

Gastric Torsion, more commonly known as bloat, occurs when there is a twist in your stomach, which causes the interruption of blood circulation and swelling of abdomen.

Bloat is a first class emergency emergency, as your dog could easily die within hours if left untreated for long. Your vet could lessen the instance of developing bloat in your Great Dane through a surgery called stomach tacking. It is the primary killer for our Great Danes, according to the Great Dane Club of America. It is notable that other deep-chest dogs could also develop this disease.

Heart Disease

Cardiomyopathy is a heart muscle disease that often affects Danes. It is noted that this disease is genetic in origin, which causes heart enlargement. Regrettably, the symptom for this disease is your Great Dane's death. But, if you notice that your pup begins to have a difficulty in breathing, take it to the vet immediately.

Your Great Dane is also susceptible to tricuspid valve disease. This is a congenital problem which happens when the heart valve doesn't work properly.

Chapter Three: The Ultimate Great Dane Health Guide

Cancer

The osteosarcoma, or bone cancer, is the most common type of cancer that can be found in your Great Dane and lymphoma.

Lymphoma usually starts as tiny lumps in different parts of the body which develops some malignant tissues. Just like other cancers, the treatment for cancer depends on the stage on which your dog is on.

Wobbler's Syndrome

Wobbler's Syndrome is the common name of the inability called cervical vertebral instability. The disease got name 'Wobbler' because this is what the affected dogs do. The disease is caused by trauma experienced by the dog. This disease develops when the dog is one year old. The symptoms of the Wobbler's Syndrome include the lethargy, odd gait, and lack of coordinationn.

It is best to have your vet diagnose your dog early to prevent further damage in its body.

Chapter Three: The Ultimate Great Dane Health Guide

Hypothyroidism

Hypothyroidism happens when there is a lack of thyroid hormone which causes weakness, hair loss, lethargy and other subtle symptoms.

If you think there is something wrong with your Great Dane, but you do not know what it is, maybe hypothyroidism is the underlying cause. You should take your dog to the vet immediately for testing. The good news is that thyroid supplementation is the treatment for this disease.

Arthritis

Arthritis can occur in any size of dog, but often associated with older adult dogs. You need to track their growth pattern and weight. Some symptoms include pain, difficulty in moving or exercising, stiffness, and limping.

Recommended Vaccinations

Just like any other babies, puppies need to be vaccinated immediately. The reason for this action is that puppies are not really immune to diseases in the outside world.

Chapter Three: The Ultimate Great Dane Health Guide

If the mother has already experienced the disease, the mother would produce the antibodies and send it into the placenta, ensuring that the puppies would receive the protection it needs especially when it is still breast feeding.

The colostrum, the mother's first milk is excreted after 36-48 hours after giving birth. Make sure that your puppies drink this milk because this is rich in antibiotics given by the mother.

The Need for Vaccination

Although the mother will provide its puppies maternal antibodies, this is not enough to help the puppies to combat the diseases in the world. A great way to help the dog combat the diseases is through vaccinations.

Types of Vaccines

The vaccines given to puppies are just like any vaccines that contains antigens. It has three categories:

Modified Live Vaccines (MLV)

This vaccine mimics a small amount of disease that would duplicate once in a dog, but would not really do anything to harm it.

Chapter Three: The Ultimate Great Dane Health Guide

Inactivated or Killed Vaccine

This variant of vaccine contains the killed whole agent. This is the oldest yet most trusted vaccine because it lasts the longest.

Recombinant Technology

This is the most advanced vaccine that has the best and freshest results possible.

The Needed Vaccines

The following vaccines help combat the following diseases:

Bordetella Bronchiseptica

Bordetella Bronchiseptica is highly communicable bacteria that can cause severe fits of coughing, vomiting, whooping, seizure, and, in some cases, death. This bacteria is the he primary why your dog will have kennel cough. But do not fret; there are nasal spray vaccines and injectable to fight off these bacteria.

Chapter Three: The Ultimate Great Dane Health Guide

Canine Distemper

Distemper is the result of a contagious and serious virus that attacks the nervous, gastrointestinal, and respiratory systems of not only dogs, but also skunks, racoons, and other animals. Distemper is spread through exposure (through coughing or sneezing) in the air from an infected animal.

Another way to transmit the virus is through sharing water and food bowls and equipment.Distemper will cause discharge from the nose and eyes, fever, coughing, twitching, fever vomiting, seizures, , diarrhea, paralysis, and, sometimes, death.

Previously, this disease is called"hardpad" because it causes the dog's foot pad to harden and thicken. Up to this day, there is no definite cure for distemper. The things you can do is to take precaution to further prevent secondary infections, symptoms of vomiting, seizures and more.

If, fortunately, the animal can withstand the symptoms, we can hope that the dog can fight off the virus inside its body. The virus can be shed by the dog after a couple of months.

Chapter Three: The Ultimate Great Dane Health Guide

Canine Hepatitis

The dog's liver, kidneys, lungs, spleen, and eyes can be infected by a highly contagious viral infection called the Canine Hepatitis. This liver disease is from a virus that is totally unrelated from the human kind of hepatitis.

Some symptoms include slight fever, congestion of the mucous member, jaundice, stomach enlargement, vomiting, and even pain in the liver. Many dogs can survive the mild form of the disease, while some forms can be fatal. There is no cure yet, but the doctor can treat all the symptoms.

Canine Parainfluenza

This is one of the viruses that can contribute to your dog's kennel cough.

Corona Virus

The Corona Virus affects the gastrointestinal system, as well can cause respiratory infections, of your dog. Symptoms include vomiting, diarrhea, and loss of appetite.

There is no definite drug that will stop the corona virus, but your doctor can help through keeping your dog warm, comfortable, hydrated, and help alleviate nausea.

Chapter Three: The Ultimate Great Dane Health Guide

Heartworm

Certain problems only occur at certain ages. At the age of 12 to 16 weeks, you need to set up an appointment with your vet and start your Great Dane with the heartworm preventative. There is no definite vaccine for this condition, but you can easily prevent it with regular medicine. Same as its name, the heartworm lodges on the pulmonary arteries (the one that sends blood to the lungs) and the right side of the heart. It can also travel to different parts of the body, and sometimes affect the kidneys and liver.

The worms can grow up to 14 inches and, if not stopped can block and injure several organs. If your dog has not experienced heartworm, there will be no visible symptoms. You can only notice coughing, becoming lethargic, losing appetite, and having difficulty in breathing if your dog has heartworms in the later stages. Other than that, infected dogs may easily get tired only after a mild exercise. Heartworms are from mosquitoes, unlike other diseases which were passed through urine, body fluids, and feces.

Chapter Three: The Ultimate Great Dane Health Guide

Kennel Cough

Kennel Cough is also known as infectious tracheobronchitis. This is a result of inflammation of the upper airways, which is caused by viral, bacterial, or other infections, such as Bordetella and canine parainfluenza, and often contains different kinds of infections working simultaneously.

The disease is usually mild which causes bouts of harsh, dry coughing. It is s severe enough to urge retching and gagging, together with a tremendous lost of appetite. It can also be deadly in some rare cases. It can easily spread among dogs if they are kept close together. You do not really need antibiotics, but is only necessary in chronic, severe cases. Cough suppressants is enough to make the dogs comfortable.

Leptospirosis

A bacteria causes leptospirosis and some dogs will not really show any symptoms. The bacteria can be seen worldwide, whether in water or soil.

It is a zoonotic disease, which means that it can easily be spread from animals to people. Some visible symptoms are infertility, fever, abdominal pain, severe weakness,

Chapter Three: The Ultimate Great Dane Health Guide

diarrhea, vomiting, loss of appetite, and lethargy, stiffness, jaundice, muscle pain, kidney failure (with or without liver failure). The sooner you give the antibiotics, the better.

Lyme Disease

There is no evident symptom for lyme disease in dogs, unlike the rash that people with lyme disease has.

Lyme disease, also called as borreliosis, is a tick-borne, infectious disease that is caused by spirochete, killer bacteria. This disease can be transmitted through ticks. You could will start limping, his lymph nodes will swell; his temperature will rise, and will lose appetite.

The disease will attack his kidney, heart, and joints that would potentially lead to neurological disorders if left untreated. If can quickly diagnose this disease, you can give your dog antibiotics, but relapse may happen, which is still easily treatable by other medication.

Parvovirus

Parvo is a highly contagious virus that wills all dogs. Unvaccinated dogs and puppies which are less than four months old are at risk to contact it. This virus mainly attacks the gastrointestinal system and leads to the loss of appetite, fever, vomiting, and often bloody, severe diarrhea.

Chapter Three: The Ultimate Great Dane Health Guide

Your dog could easily die within 48 to 72 hours due to extreme dehydration, so you need to contact your vet immediately. At this point, there is no certain cure for this virus. You better keep your dog hydrated to control the other symptoms until the immune system could beat the illness.

Rabies

Rabies is a viral disease of all mammals which invades the central nervous system. This virus can cause paralysis, excessive drooling, anxiety, hallucinations, headache, fear of water, and death.

Rabies is transmitted through the bite of a rabid animal. You should treat the infection within hours, or else, death may be seen. Most states and countries require you to vaccinate your dog against rabies. These are just some of the diseases that vaccines may be able to stop, talk to your vet to know more about these things. With these in mind, you should decide to have your puppies vaccinated as soon as possible.

Chapter Three: The Ultimate Great Dane Health Guide

Puppy Vaccination Schedule:

Age	Recommended Vaccines	Additional Vaccines
Six to eight weeks	Parainfluenza, distemper, measles	Bordetella
10 to 12 weeks	DHPP	Coronavirus, lyme disease, bordetella, leptospirosis
12 - 24 weeks	Rabies	none
14 - 16 weeks	DHPP	Leptospirosis, coronavirus, lyme disease
12 to 16 months	Rabies, DHPP	Bordetella, coronavirus, leptotspirosis, lyme disease
1 year above	DHPP	Bordetella, coronavirus, leptotspirosis, lyme disease
Yearly Vaccine	Rabies	none

Chapter Three: The Ultimate Great Dane Health Guide

Vaccination Tips

- Ask your vet when you can have your puppy vaccinated.
- The first shot of vaccine needs to be given during six to eight weeks after birth. This will continue until you have completed four rounds of vaccinations.
- Rabies vaccination should be given to 16 to 26 week old puppies, then yearly after the initial vaccine.
- Get your puppies additional booster shots to fight off common diseases.
- Be updated with the vaccines, boosters, and shots of your puppies or dog so you can know when to follow up for additional shots.

Chapter Three: The Ultimate Great Dane Health Guide

Chapter Four: Fact or Bluff? What to Believe?

Dogs are one of the top choices if you want to have your own household pet. You can take care of it just like your own child. A good example of an amazing household pet is the Great Dane. Relative to its name, the Great Dane stands majestically. It is great for owners who like to walk and run around the block and can provide obedience training for the dog. In this part, we will give you exciting facts and trivia that you do not know about the Great Dane! Aside from that, we will debunk several myths to break off the Great Dane stereotype in your mind.

Chapter Four: Fact or Bluff? What to Believe?

Fun Great Dane Facts

Here, we will be giving you fun facts about your Great Dane. Some are mildly believable, while some are just outrageous!

The Name Does Not Really Suggest its Origin

Although the breed's name is Great Dane, the dogs have ties to Germany, not Denmark.

Some people believe the name was coined when French naturalist Georges-Louis Leclerc, Comte de Buffon saw the breed when he was travelling in Denmark in the early 1700s. He called the dog 'le Grande Danois' or the Great Dane. After that, the name just stuck.

Great Danes Were Once Used to Hunt Boars

This canine is a crossbreed of the Irish wolfhound and the old English mastiff. Initially Great Danes were used to track down wild boars, which mean the Danes needed to be physically strong as well as brave.

Chapter Four: Fact or Bluff? What to Believe?

The Great Danes were powerful hunters because they were quick and deadly. They have aggressive behavior which is the total opposite of the temperament the Great Danes have today.

People do not really know the real history of the Danes, but they do know that the Great Dane's ancestor may have come across with ancient Egyptians. There are several dog images that can be seen on Egyptian monuments. Great Danes were also seen in Tibetian, Greek, and Chinese literature.

Great Danes are the Gentle Giants in the Doggy World

Great Danes, today, are also known as gentle giants. When people stopped using the Great Danes in hunting boars, the breed evolved to becoming show dogs.

Right now, the Great Danes prefer to have a leisurely lifestyle rather than fighting for their lives. In fact, having Great Danes as pets has become a great addition in one's family.

Chapter Four: Fact or Bluff? What to Believe?

The Reason Why Scooby Doo is a Great Dane

Great Danes were initially thought to shoo evil spirits and ghosts. Just like the breed it is based from, Scooby Doo is perfect with those kids because they are constantly competing with spirit. Although this was not the original plan of the creators, it is just a 'happy accident'.

The producers chose the Great Dane because they have they decided that Scooby needs to be large cowardly dog. The Dane was against the sheepdog, they did not choose the latter because the sheep dog already appeared in the Archie comics.

They Are Not the Tallest In Their Family

We think that Great Dane is the tallest among all the dog breeds. Typically, the Great Dane stands at 2.5 to 2.8 feet. Unfortunately, the Irish Wolfhound is taller than the Danes.

Chapter Four: Fact or Bluff? What to Believe?

A Dane Was Awarded Not One... But Two Blue Cross Medals!

In recent history, a hero dog was awarded with not only one but two blue cross medals! Julianna, truly a Great Dane, peed on a bomb to diffuse it. How did it happen? Julianna was rudely awakened when the bomb fell on the house she lived on. What a nice revenge, right? Other than that, Julianna also alerted the cops when her owner's shoe shop was on fire.

A Great Dane in the Navy

Just Nuisance, another Great Dane, is the only dog to be officially enlisted in the Navy. He was born in the late 1930s, later on; he grew up in the United Services Institute.

In the US Institute, he had formed an attachment with Navy sailors that commanded the base. The Great Dane truly liked to ride the train with his new friends; unfortunately the train conductors were quite unhappy with having a dog stowaway, because it is quite difficult to hide a big dog in the train. The management threatened to put Just Nuisance down if he continues to ride the rain for free.

Chapter Four: Fact or Bluff? What to Believe?

The Sailors truly loved travelling with the Great Dane, so they decided to enlist Just Nuisance in the Navy. Sailors have free train rides, which means, Just Nuisance can also enjoy the train rides with his friends without the fear of being put down.

Although he never went to sea, he kept his friends company during events. Eventually he married another named Adinda. Just Nuisance was buried with full naval honors when he passed away.

The Great Dane as Official State Dog

Pennsylvania truly love the Great Dane, because of this the Dane became the official state dog of Pennsylvania. There are several paintings of the Great Dane in the Governor's reception room, especially with the state's founder - William Penn.

They Will Grow Up Fast.

Great Dane has a starting weight of one to two pounds. In less than a year, they can weigh as much as 100 pounds! They continue to grow bigger (and heavier) until the age of three.

Chapter Four: Fact or Bluff? What to Believe?

Great Danes and Goats Are BFFs

Who would have thought that a dog and a goat could be bff? In 2010, Minnelli (a goat) unlatched the gate of Judy's (Great Dane) home. They eloped in a nearby Dallas-area chapel where they met a three-legged yellow labrador named Lucky.

The three animals captured the hearts of the American people and are inseparable. Unfortunately, the original owners of Judy and Minnelli cannot really keep the three animals together, so they decided to give them up for adoption. Luckily, a couple took the trio as their own.

The Great Dane is Pretty Popular

The Great Dane ranks 15th in the Most Popular Dog Breed category according to the American Kennel Club. The Danes have nine approved colors with three approved markings. Other than that, the AKC recognized the Great Dane in 1887.

Chapter Four: Fact or Bluff? What to Believe?

They Can Live Wherever They Like

Although people might think that you need to regularly walk your Dane, it is actually a myth. Danes can live in small spaces. A plus factor is that they do not bark too much so you won't have your neighbours banging on your wall.

The Great Dane as the Tallest Dog

Although they are not the tallest breed, the tallest dog is a Great Dane. Zeus held the Guinness World Record as the tallest dog. Sadly he died in the year 2004.

The Great Dane Has One of the Shortest Lives

The Great Dane is one of the breeds that have the shortest life span. They can only live 6-8 years. They are much shorter than small dogs such as Chihuahuas.

Looks Can Be Truly Deceiving

Many people are quite scared of the Great Dane due to its size. They are afraid that this massive dog will attack them immediately. However, the Great Dane is one of the most loving, affectionate, and loyal breed of dog. They can be compared to giant teddy bears.

Chapter Four: Fact or Bluff? What to Believe?

Other than that, you should not really be afraid that it might attack children, because they love children! However, you should keep a close supervision to small kids. Great Danes are a great companion for you. You won't ever feel sad whenever you are with this very big teddy bear.

Here are some variations of the name 'Great Dane' in different languages:

- Catalan: danès
- Finnish: tanskandoggi
- French: dogue allemand
- German: Deutsche Dogge or Dänische Dogge
- Hebrew: דני ענק
- Italian: danese or alano
- Japanese: グレート・デーン (gurēto dēn)
- Lithuanian: vokiečių dogas
- Mandarin: 大丹狗 (dàdāngǒu)
- Norwegian:
    o Bokmål: grand danois m
    o Nynorsk: grand danois m
-

Chapter Four: Fact or Bluff? What to Believe?

- Polish: dog niemiecki

- Portuguese: dogue, alemão, dinamarquês

- Russian: да́тский дог m (dátskij dog)

- Spanish: dogo alemán, dogo danés, gran danés, alano alemán

- Swedish: grand danois

- Valencian: danés

Myths Surrounding the Great Dane

Every fact has a myth that accompanies it. Great Danes are also a victim of these myths. In this portion, we will break off some myths that people usually tag the Great Dane with. Read on to know more.

Myth: The Great Dane is not suited for Small Spaces

Although Great Dane is a gigantic dog, almost any dog can live in any space possible! You can still get a Great Dane yet live in a small apartment. You just need give him the required exercise that he needs. Just run, play, and walk with him and he will surely relax in any space that you will give it.

Chapter Four: Fact or Bluff? What to Believe?

Myth: Great Danes are Great Guard Dogs

You might thing that big dog equates to a great big guard dog. This myth is truly a myth. Your dog's temperament will heavily depend on how you train it.

Your Great Dane will be vicious if you let him be, however, they can be your cuddly furry friend if you want him to be.

Myth: Great Danes are Truly Vicious

This is closely related to the myth above. When people see big dogs such as Great Danes or Mastiff, they think that these are vicious killing animals. However, most mastiff and Danes are truly lovable creatures. You should not judge a dog by its size. There are some smaller breeds which are more vicious than the Danes.

Myth: Great Danes Can't Be Lapdogs

Although you really do not want a big dog to sit on your lap, Great Danes truly love to be lapdogs. If you think the Great Dane does not want to be cuddled, you must be novice owner. This gigantic dog always wants to be near its owner, and sometimes be on your lap rather than staying on

Chapter Four: Fact or Bluff? What to Believe?

the floor. It is best that you practice to have 200 pounds on your lap as soon as possible.

Myth: Great Danes Can't Be With Kids

This is really quite contrary than what is happening in the world. Many giant and large breeds, such as the Great Dane, love playing with children.

The Great Dane really likes to have a family bonding time with other. Children are small and fragile creatures and the Great Dane could easily wipe out the school project or a kid's board game, or even kill a small child himself. However, this is not always the case. Remember that the dog's temperament relies heavily on how you raise your dog. If you raise him to be vicious and wild - no one could go near it. But, naturally, Great Danes love to cuddle with their human and small children.

Myth: Great Danes Will Just Get Fat over the Years to Come

This one is a big myth. Not all Great Danes are destined to be fat. Although they will weigh up to 100 pounds, this can be easily taken care of by proper and regular exercise and less food intake.

Chapter Four: Fact or Bluff? What to Believe?

These are some myths that surround our favourite furry friends. Now that we have broken these myths, we are ready to move forward and learn more. Let's continue our journey!

Chapter Four: Fact or Bluff? What to Believe?

Chapter Five: What Will My Great Dane Eat? A Primer

A healthy dog is a happy and active dog. Feeding your Great Dane might not be an easy task, but you could learn a lot from their feeding and eating habits. Just like humans, there are many factors that could affect your Great Dane's food requirement, such as hormonal changes, diseases, gender, age, and the exercise that they have. You just consult your vet immediately if there is a big change in mood and activity of your dog such as diarrhea, vomiting, or lethargy.

Chapter Five: What Will My Great Dane Eat? A Primer

Feeding your pet will heavily depend on the factors given above. If you need to follow a strict budget, you should still give your dog a balanced diet that will ensure your Great Dane's good health. If you plan to buy the first dog food that you see on the market, without researching, will result to your dog not really liking the food that you will give it. Also, some manufacturers do not really give the essential information and nutritional needs of your puppy and your adult dog.

In this portion, we will give you all the health information as possible, as well as restriction, nutritional needs, and feeding tips and tricks. We will also be listing down foods that will be harmful for your pet The Great Dane. Make sure you take note of all the things here so you will know what to buy in your pet store or grocery.

The Nutritional Needs of Dogs

In order to promote good health and growth to your Great Dane, you should give him a balanced diet. You need to look out for the best quality of dog food that will cover all the nutritional need, special needs, and etc. Just like humans, dogs have different nutritional needs that need to be sufficed.

Chapter Five: What Will My Great Dane Eat? A Primer

These nutrients are used to create a happy and healthy life for him. Make sure you take note of these things when buying pet food, vitamins and treats. There are the important nutrients your dog needs to have a happy life:

Water

Dog is also made up of 60% - 70% water, just like us. When there is a decrease in your dog's body water, it could lead to serious sickness or even death. You need to have an accessible water bowl for your pet whenever it wants to drink. We are not always by our dog's side to know when they are thirsty. Other than that, they walk, jump, and play around when we are sleeping, with a water bowl close by, they can drink whenever they like to.

Canned food has 80% moisture while the pet food only has 10%. You better have water readily available for dogs so they will be always hydrated.

Carbohydrate

Carbohydrate is used for its glucose content, although dogs do not really need carbohydrates in their daily diet. You can find carbohydrates in oatmeal and brown rice. Do not give your dog's corn and soy because they have low

Chapter Five: What Will My Great Dane Eat? A Primer

quality carbohydrates and are not really needed by your furry friend.

Protein

Proteins are needed by the cell because it is its primary component. Other than that proteins make up our enzymes, hormones, tissues, organs, and antibodies.

Our Great Dane needs protein to help in their body's growth, repair, reproduction, and maintenance. Some good sources of protein are lamb, eggs, chicken, beef, fish, while vegetables contain only a few.

Minerals

Minerals can't be cultivated by the animals on its own. We should be the one to introduce Minerals in their diet. Minerals are needed because its boosts and strengthens one's teeth and bones, and balances their metabolism. Important minerals needed by the dog are: iron, potassium, calcium, copper, phosphorus, and sodium.

Chapter Five: What Will My Great Dane Eat? A Primer

Fats

Fats are the purest source of energy. It gives the most amount of energy than carbohydrates or protein. You should provide your Great Dane a balance of omega-6 and omega-3 fatty acids that will give your pet a healthy coat and glowing skin. Other than that, fats provide protection and insulation. If you fail to provide these to your pet, it could result to skin problems and serious illnesses.

Just like protein, you can get fats from animal-based sources like fish oil and chicken fat instead of plant-based sources like canola oil and flax seed.

Vitamins

Vitamins are needed for a great and healthy metabolism just like humans. Dogs could not produce their own vitamins so we need to be the one to introduce the vitamin in our diet.

Although it is essential to give vitamins, it is quite unnecessary to give them extra supplements unless given by the veterinarian. Your dog could be poisoned if given a large dosage of vitamins. The needed vitamins by the Great Dane are vitamin A, vitamin C, vitamin D and vitamin E.

Chapter Five: What Will My Great Dane Eat? A Primer

How to Select a Healthy Dog Food Brand

Feeding your pet is a difficult task. You need to find the perfect dog food that would suit the need of your pet. You need to find the perfect food that your pet would enjoy while still being in your budget. You need to keep in mind that the dog food should give plenty of nutrients and won't upset his stomach. This will create a happy and healthy dog in the future.

These are just some of the dog food brands that we recommend:

Gentle Giants Medium Natural Dog Food Grain Free with Salmon, Fruits, Vegetables, Vitamins and Minerals

- Complete nutrition for any age: puppies, adults, seniors. Suitable for big, small, medium, or any times of dog!

- Your pup would surely enjoy this, beginning from its puppy years until its senior era.

- Provides NON GMO for your pets. The tomato-vegetable pomace with watercress, spinach, parsley,

Chapter Five: What Will My Great Dane Eat? A Primer

lettuce, betts, carrots, tomato, celery, cranberries, blueberries, and apples are not Genetically Modified.

- It is not greasy. Remember, if your food is greasy, it will not be good for your dog.

CRAVE Grain Free High Protein Dry Dog Food

- Contains almost one pound of food for any dog age!
- Made with high quality real lamb that your dog will truly enjoy.
- Made with 34% protein that is truly needed by your Great Dane
- Grain free but a great source of quality carbohydrate sources for energy
- Crafted with quality ingredients: NO chicken by-product meal, wheat, corn, or soy protein, and NO preservatives, colors, or even artificial flavors.

Holistic Select Natural Dry Dog Food

- This dry food is focused on probiotics, digestive enzymes, botanical, prebiotics, and natural fibers that truly support and give a unique digestive health system

Chapter Five: What Will My Great Dane Eat? A Primer

- This is suited for large dog. Made with everyday complete and balanced diet needed by your pet.

- Contains all natural, premium ingredients that is not made from by products, wheat, wheat gluten, fillers, flavors, and artificial colors.

CANIDAE All Life Stages Large Breed Adult Dog Food Made With Duck Meal, Brown Rice & Lentils

- Gives the best protein through a calcium and phosphorus in a duck meal

- No corn, wheat, or soy were used in making this premium pet food

- Formulated for large breeds

Rachael Ray Nutrish Natural Dry Dog Food, Turkey, Brown Rice & Venison Recipe

- Its number one ingredient is the US Beef
- Contains Prebiotics that helps in natural and healthy digestion
- No Artificial preservatives and flavors

Chapter Five: What Will My Great Dane Eat? A Primer

- No Poultry By-Product! Made with all fresh ingredient
- Packed with added vitamin and minerals

EUKANUBA Adult Dry Dog Food

- Eukanuba uses chicken in its food. Chicken is used to maintain lean muscles.
- Eukanuba gives a great fiber system, made from prebiotic FOS and natural ingedients, that promotes healthy digestion and nutrient absorption.
- Uses glucosamine and chondroitin to help support and promote healthy joints
- Have optimal levels of omega-6 and -3 fatty acids to promote glowing and healthy looking skin

Iams PROACTIVE HEALTH Adult Dry Dog Food

- Uses Chicken that helps maintain and promote healthy joints and bones
- Has glucosamine and chondroitin sulfate that can help prevent osteoarthritis
- Promotes strong muscles using quality protein
- Has a blend of fiber and prebiotics to promote and maintain good digestion

Chapter Five: What Will My Great Dane Eat? A Primer

Taste of the Wild Grain Free High Protein Natural Dry Dog Food

- Made from real bison meat to have an optimal amino acid profile, to give a protein rich meal to promote lean and strong muscles.
- Made with minerals and minerals, fruits and vegetables. To have antioxidants and create a great skin and coat
- No preservatives were used in making the dog food.

BLUE Life Protection Formula Adult Dry Dog Food

- Made with protein rich, deboned, delicious chicken
- It has fruits, veggies, and whole grains
- Contains a great blend of minerals, vitamins and antioxidants
- No by-product was used in making this food, as well as preservatives and artificial coloring.

Chapter Five: What Will My Great Dane Eat? A Primer

Here are some guidelines for you to choose the best dog food for your pet:

Read and Understand the Food Packaging

Food packaging contains all the necessary information about the dog food that you will find. You need to remember that water is a vital part of that dog food, and might tone down other nutrients with it. It could tone down the nutrients up to 20%!

Some brands might say that their dog food contains "beef" or "chicken" but are only by-products. Read carefully to choose the best for your beloved pet.

Get to know your dog

Your dog's temperament will determine the kind of food it needs. Also, you need to know the amount your dogs need to avoid obesity.

Mothers and their puppies need more food as they do more that requires them to have higher energy source, while older dogs need less because they do not really do much. Active dogs need more food than your ordinary lap dogs. Know the personality so you will know how much and what kind of food you need to give to your dog.

Chapter Five: What Will My Great Dane Eat? A Primer

It Contains What?

Understanding the content will help you determine if the food is really suited for your dog.

Do not introduce new kinds of diet to your dog (such as vegan or vegetarian) as they naturally omnivores and might have a hard time in coping with the new food in the mix. Also, choose the brand which gives or lists down the meat first, as they will contain the highest water content. There are many sources of meat available, such as our tissues, esophagus, and skeletal muscles.

How much is truly enough?

Some of your dog food might say "complete and balanced nutrition" you should still see if this will be enough for your pet.

You can look up the Association of American Feed Control Officials (AAFCO)'s standard. The membership in this organization is only voluntarily, but you can see that they have set a high standard for manufacturers to follow, which is fitting for their consumers.

Chapter Five: What Will My Great Dane Eat? A Primer

Should you switch it up?

If you notice that your dog does not like its food. It is best to try and mix it up and find another dog food for the meantime, although, you might need to talk to your vet first. Switching dog foods is not really a bad idea, but do not ever indulge them into getting or trying new fads such as gluten free.

List Down Everything

You need to have a lot of research in order to find the best dog food for your puppy. Research all the materials well, know the manufacturers, ingredients, and etc. List down the pros and cons of your choice, whatever makes you happy - but it immediately.

Tips for Feeding Your Pet

We have already established that feeding your pet is a tedious task; you might give too little or just too much. The Great Danes are a large breed of dog, you just need to give them the exact amount of food or else they will either be obese or be underweight.

Chapter Five: What Will My Great Dane Eat? A Primer

You can start by following the recommended feeding guidelines in your dog food; see if your dog reacts positively or negatively with this trait. If your dog becomes lighter, add more food, or if your dog tremendously gains weight, lessen the food that you will give it. Also remember to take note of how many times you need to feed your dog.

We have already discussed how much you should feed your puppy and adult Great Dane. Follow the recommended cups daily and it will have a happy life.

Toxic Foods to Avoid

You might be tempted to give your dog whatever it likes. But, certain human foods are actually toxic for your dog.

You should give something you are 100% will help your dog. We will give you a list of food that you should avoid giving your dog. Contact the Pet Poison Control immediately if your Great Dane accidentally eats it at (888) 426 – 4435.

- Alcohol
- Cherry pits
- Chocolate

Chapter Five: What Will My Great Dane Eat? A Primer

- Coffee
- Potato leaves/stems
- Rhubarb leaves
- Tea
- Tomato leaves/stem
- Xylitol
- Yeast do
- Apple seeds
- Avocado
- ugh
- Walnuts
- Garlic
- Grapes/raisins
- Hops
- Macadamia nuts
- Mold
- Mushrooms
- Mustard seeds
- Onions/leeks
- Peach pits

Chapter Five: What Will My Great Dane Eat? A Primer

Chapter Six: Breeding Your Great Dane

Having two Great Danes at once, especially of opposite genders, is a big and difficult responsibility. You should keep in mind that there will be a big possibility for breeding, especially if you keep them together. You can create a Great Dane lineage and develop several generations. You could also be a breeder and sell some of the puppies. Just take good care as there are a lot of things to do that will require your time, money, effort, and love for the dogs.

Chapter Six: Breeding Your Great Dane

Just like any parent, you need to prepare yourself physically, emotionally, and financially. Some of the puppies might die during or after the birthing process so you need to prepare yourself for loss. Aside from that buying two pets at once is a big investment, other than that, you need to give them enough nutrients and vitamins during its developmental years.

In this sixth chapter, we will give you detailed explanation on how to breed your Great Dane. We will also be giving you tips on how to raise your pups yourself. Raising puppies might be difficult but they are just like babies who we need to take care of, especially during the first few days. Prepare everything that you can, because this will be a difficult task.

Basic Dog Breeding Information

Breeding any pet is a big deal. You should make up your mind that you can do it before it even happens. You need to be financially prepared before the start of the breeding process. You can set up a Great Dane family, give it as presents, or even sell it for a few bucks.

Some people might think that breeding dogs is just an easy task. There are some costs that you need to prepare, such as puppy vitamins, overall care, and even prenatal

Chapter Six: Breeding Your Great Dane

vitamins. You will be very lucky if you will create a fortune out of this process. You might be discouraged now, but the process of breeding your pet is such a wonderful task.

If you do not plan to breed your pet, have him or her spayed or neutered immediately. For females, you should have them spayed before the first heat. Remember that spaying and neutering before the 6 month mark will reduce the risk of cancers and other serious diseases. However, if you do not like this process, better keep your dogs away from each other. This will prevent accidental mating between the two of them.

Mating Behavior of Dogs

First thing you need to understand about mating is the "estrus cycle", also known as the "heat" period, in which female dogs will experience twice a year. This cycle lasts will 14 to 21 days on average and it occurs about every half year once it becomes regular. However, some dogs take years before having a regular cycle.

Your female dog will excrete bloody discharge when the cycle, or might not develop until the seventh day. Other than that, you will notice that there is the swelling of the

Chapter Six: Breeding Your Great Dane

vulva. As the days go by, the discharge becomes lighter in color until it becomes watery and pink.

Aside from those signs, your female dog will also start urinating more than usual. They will create a marking behavior to attract male dogs. A male dog will when a female is in heat even from afar; you need to keep your female away from them when in heat.

When in heat, you need to keep your Great Dane ou on a leash and closely supervise all the time - especially during walks outside. Never let your female Great Dane alone in any locations such as in a dog park or any other location where there is a male dog present, especially if you want to breed your dog specifically for another dog.

Another tell-tale sign for dog's fertility is when its vulva becomes light in color and watery. She will, then, ovulate which happens typically during days 11-15 of the cycle. This is a right time for you to have the male dog with your female dog.

Remember, you don't introduce the dogs too early because your female might not really like the male. Or, you can also try mating them after two to three days of initial meeting. Great Danes are capable of conceiving at any point during her reproductive cycle. The sperm will survive in the bitch's reproductive tract for as long as five days.

Chapter Six: Breeding Your Great Dane

Tips for Breeding Your Great Dane

You have now decided that you want to breed your Great Dane. However, there are still things for you to remember when mating them. It is more complicated that just mating them. Here are some points to remember when mating your adult dogs. Keep these in mind as they are essential to your breeding process:

- **Size:** You need to make sure that both male and female are same in size and have the same pelvic breadth. Your female might have a hard time with a bigger male counterpart.

- **Age:** You should only breed female dogs after its eighth month and male dogs after its seventh month. The best age for female to carry puppies is two years. Breeding early will give deficiencies as well as illnesses for the future pups.

- **Learn Their History:** Make sure you have enough idea for both the male and female dog. Dig and research to know more about them. Do not just breed them for the sake of breeding them.

Chapter Six: Breeding Your Great Dane

- **How much?** You need to have enough budget during the breeding, pregnancy, and post natal of the puppies and mother. It is not cheap to take care of puppies, so you need to be prepared no matter what happens.

- **Be emotionally prepared:** There are instances when your puppy might die during birth. You need to be ready for possible death scenarios.

- **In it for the long run:** Not all puppies will be sold. You need to take care of the litters that will be left with you. Do not just abandon them because you do not have enough budget.

- **Don't overbreed:** Do not tire your female dog in breeding too much. Let her rest before you breed her for the next batch.

The Labor Process of Your Great Dane

Helping your pet to give birth can be a stressful but fun filled experience, and will be very rewarding. Your Great Dane might give birth at around nine weeks. Before that mark, you should prepare all the materials needed for delivery. Prepare a room for the birthing process; this will help your female dog give birth. You might need to help your dog in giving birth, so you need to be prepared for that.

Preparing for Birth

- You need to have a box within your home. This will become the mini shelter for the pups and a place for the mother to take care of its puppies.

- Have blankets all over the box. This will provide the needed comfort for your Great Dane. Aside from that, have a lamp near the box to give off heat for the puppies. However, you must make sure you place aluminum foil outside the lamp to prevent the accidents involving the puppies' eyes.

- Accustom your pet in the box. Make her feel that that is her home.

- Remove any fur that might block the delivery.

The Birthing Process

- Have a laundry basket near the box. The basket will serve as a holding area for the newborn puppies. This

Chapter Six: Breeding Your Great Dane

will ensure that the mother could freely walk while she is delivering the puppies.

- Let your dog give birth on its own. You just remove the birthing sac from their faces only if the mother won't do it.

- Tie a thread on the umbilical cord and have another one in an inch apart, then cut the cord between two threads.

- Let the Great Dane lick the puppy's face. This will start the blood flow. If the mother can't do it, hold the puppy and rub it with a towel.

- Wrap the puppy in a towel before placing it in a basket.

- Let there be bonding time between the mother and her puppies. Have the available food and water ready.

These are just some of the birthing process that you will go through. Be ready as you need to help your female dog deliver its puppies.

Chapter Seven: The Great Dane's Ultimate Cheat Sheet

You have gone through lot while reading this book; it is now time to summarize everything we have discussed! You can look up more information about our beloved Great Dane online, but, this portion will be your cheat sheet on all things Great Dane! Take note of these things as they will become very handy in one of these days.

Chapter Seven: The Great Dane's Ultimate Cheat Sheet

Basic Great Dane Information

Origin: Germany

Pedigree: people consider the breed as a crossbreed Irish Wolfhound and English Mastiff

Breed Size: big size (working group)

Body Type and Appearance: Has a big, bulky body. It stands tall and alert for intruders.

Group: American Kennel Club, Westminster Kennel Club, Great Dane Club of America

Height: 76-68 cm (male) and 71-81 cm (female)

Weight: 54-90 kg (male) and 45-59 kg (female)

Coat Length: short-hair

Coat Texture: glossy

Color: brindle, fawn, black, harlequin, blue, and mantle

Temperament: devoted, reserved, gentle, confident, loving, friendly

Strangers: friendly around strangers

Other Dogs: both genders get along with other dogs

Other Pets: gets along well with other pets

Chapter Seven: The Great Dane's Ultimate Cheat Sheet

Training: due to its size, you need to establish authority over your Great Dane

Exercise Needs: needs 30 to 60 minutes of daily exercise.

Health Conditions: generally healthy but can contract common illnesses such as Canine hip dysplasia, Pattelar, ear infection, and others

Lifespan: average 8 - 10 years.

Habitat Requirements

Recommended Accessories: crate, dog bed, food/water dishes, toys, collar, leash, harness, grooming supplies

Collar and Harness: sized by weight

Grooming Supplies: nail clipper, brush

Grooming Frequency: occasionall

Energy Level: alert, active

Exercise Requirements: frequent exercises is needed

Crate: not that much recommended

Crate Size: large

Food/Water: preferably ceramic bowls or stainless steel

Chapter Seven: The Great Dane's Ultimate Cheat Sheet

Toys: start with an assortment, see what the dog likes; include some mentally stimulating toys

Training: loves training

Nutritional Needs

Nutritional Needs: carbohydrate, fats, water,, vitamins, minerals, and protein

Calorie Needs: modified for weight, age, gender, and level of activity

Amount to Feed (puppy): based on the age/ month

Amount to Feed (adult): once to thrice a day, around seven to ten cups

Important Ingredients: digestible carbohydrates (oats, barley and, rice), animal fats, fresh animal protein (turkey, eggs, chicken, beef, lamb)

Important Minerals: calcium, magnesium, iron, copper, phosphorus, potassium, and manganese

Important Vitamins: Vitamin A, Vitamin C, Vitamin D, Vitamin D

Chapter Seven: The Great Dane's Ultimate Cheat Sheet

Certifications: AAFCO statement of nutritional adequacy; protein at top of ingredients list; no artificial flavors, dyes, preservatives

Breeding Information

Age of First Heat: around five to eight months (or even earlier)

Heat (Estrus) Cycle: 15 to 21 days

Frequency: once or twice a year

Greatest Fertility: 11 to 15 days into the cycle

Gestation Period: 50 to 60 days

Pregnancy Detection: can be seen after 24 to 25 days, best to wait for 45 days

Feeding Pregnant Dogs: normal diet until it reaches its fourth to fifth week

Signs of Labor: dropping of temperature below 100° to 102°F (37.7° to 38.8°C), could be as low as 98°F (36.6°C); dog will begin nesting in a dark, quiet place

Contractions: period of ten minutes in waves of two to three; then will rest

Chapter Seven: The Great Dane's Ultimate Cheat Sheet

Whelping: puppies are born in half hour increments. Then follows a ten to thirty minutes of forceful straining

Puppies: born with eyes and ears closed; eyes open at three weeks, teeth develop at ten weeks

Litter Size: average 4 to 6 puppies

Size at Birth: about 100 pounds or more

Weaning: start offering puppy food soaked in water at six weeks; can be fully weaned at 8 weeks

Socialization: start early to prevent vicious tendencies

Photo Credits

Page 1 Photo by user mtajmr via Pixabay.com,

https://pixabay.com/en/dog-great-dane-3181898/

Page 14 Photo by user mtajmr via Pixabay.com,

https://pixabay.com/en/great-dane-dog-h-head-2914317/

Page 20 Photo by user mtajmr via Pixabay.com,

https://pixabay.com/en/great-dane-portrait-dog-2793816/

Page 46 Photo by user mtajmr via Pixabay.com,

https://pixabay.com/en/dog-run-great-dane-3181899/

Page 78 Photo by user monnieblazkova via Pixabay.com,

https://pixabay.com/en/dog-head-nature-snout-great-dane-2869572/

Page 91 Photo by user mtajmr via Pixabay.com,

https://pixabay.com/en/dog-great-dane-puppy-snow-ještěd-2098715/

Page 107 Photo by user sergeljeanette via Pixabay.com,

https://pixabay.com/en/dog-great-dane-old-animal-pet-2514968/

Page 116 Photo by user fb2013 via Pixabay.com,

https://pixabay.com/en/dog-great-dane-ears-happy-2803935/

References

Great Dane Breed Intro - All-About-Great-Danes.com

http://www.all-about-great-danes.com/great-dane-breed.html

Great Dane - Dogtime.com

http://dogtime.com/dog-breeds/great-dane#/slide/1

Great Dane: History and Health – PetWave.com

http://www.petwave.com/Dogs/Breeds/Great-Dane/Overview.aspx

Great Dane – American Kennel Organization

http://www.akc.org/dog-breeds/great-dane/

Great Dane Growth Chart Depicting the Developmental Stages of This Dog - Dogappy.com

https://dogappy.com/great-dane-growth-chart

Great Dane Life Span – American Kennel Organization

http://www.akc.org/expert-advice/health/general-health/great-dane-life-span/

How Much and Often to Feed a Great Dane - Cuteness.com

https://www.cuteness.com/blog/content/how-much-and-often-to-feed-a-great-dane

Great Dane - Temperament & Personality - Petwave.com

http://www.petwave.com/Dogs/Breeds/Great-Dane/Personality.aspx

Great Dane - YourPureBredPuppy.com

http://www.yourpurebredpuppy.com/reviews/greatdanes.html

Great Dane Price: Why They're Absolutely Worth It! (2017) – HerPup.com

https://herepup.com/how-much-do-great-danes-cost/

Eye Problems in Great Danes - Symptoms and Treatment - CanineHealthAnswers.blogspot.com

http://caninehealthanswers.blogspot.com/2016/03/eye-care-for-great-dane.html

The Medical Problems in Great Danes – The Nest

https://pets.thenest.com/medical-problems-great-danes-5016.html

First-Year Puppy Vaccinations; A Complete Guide – American Kennel Organization

http://www.akc.org/expert-advice/health/puppy-health/puppy-shots-complete-guide/

10 Larger Than Life Facts About Great Danes Everyone Should Know - 3milliondogs.com

https://3milliondogs.com/dogbook/10-larger-than-life-facts-about-great-danes-everyone-should-know/

7 Myths You Shouldn't Believe About Big Dogs - VetStreet.com

http://www.vetstreet.com/our-pet-experts/7-myths-you-shouldnt-believe-about-big-dogs

Dog Nutrition Tips – ASPCA.org

https://www.aspca.org/pet-care/dog-care/dog-nutrition-tips